I SPY
A SCHOOL BUS

For Karin and Sam Rees,
with thanks to Dan
—J.M.

For Melanie Word
— W.W.

Text copyright © 2003 by Jean Marzollo.
"Tiny Toys," "Odds & Ends," "Bulletin Board," "At the Beach," and "Blocks" from
I Spy © 1992 by Walter Wick; "The Mysterious Monster" and "A Whale of a Tale"
from *I Spy Mystery* © 1993 by Walter Wick; "City Blocks" and "Yikes!" from *I Spy Fantasy*
© 1994 by Walter Wick; "Mapping" from *I Spy School Days* © 1995 by Walter Wick.

Library of Congress Cataloging-in-Publication Data is available.

ISBN-13: 978-0-439-52473-5
ISBN-10: 0-439-52473-3

63

22/0

Printed in the U.S.A. 40 • This edition first printing, July 2008

I SPY

A SCHOOL BUS

Riddles by Jean Marzollo
Photographs by Walter Wick

SCHOLASTIC INC.

I spy

a bus,

  two trees,

a green star,

 a hopscotch game,

and a smile on a car.

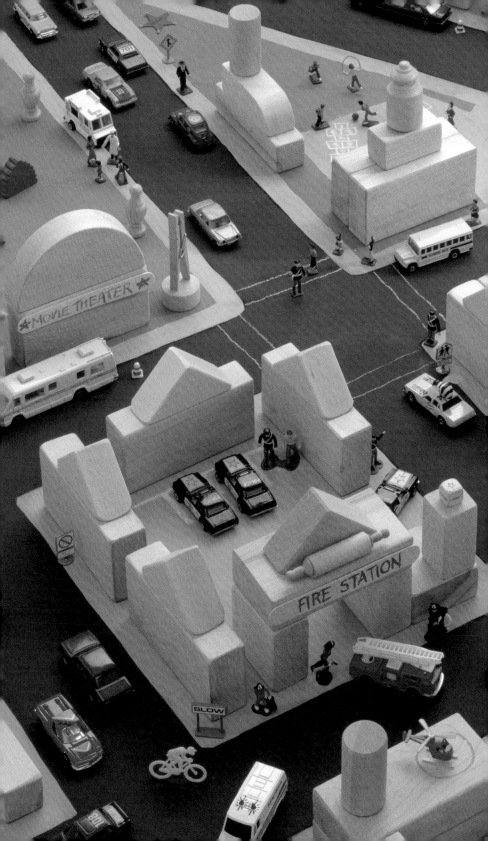

I spy

glasses

 a lobster,

five fish,

 a chick in a boat,

 and a penny for a wish.

I spy
corn,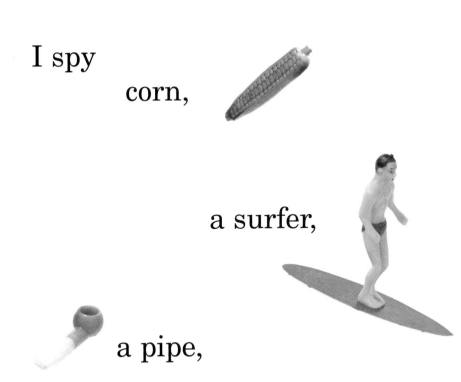

a surfer,

a pipe,

a pink stingray,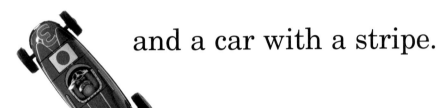

and a car with a stripe.

I spy

a screwdriver,

 a face that's small,

scissors,

a comb,

and a little football.

I spy  a hammer,

a nut,

 a deer,

two little stars,

 and a glass
that is clear.

I spy

a green hat,

 a boxing glove,

a duck,

and a rainbow
high above.

I spy

 five cards,

a button that's red,

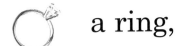 a ring,

 a badge,

 and a crown for a head.

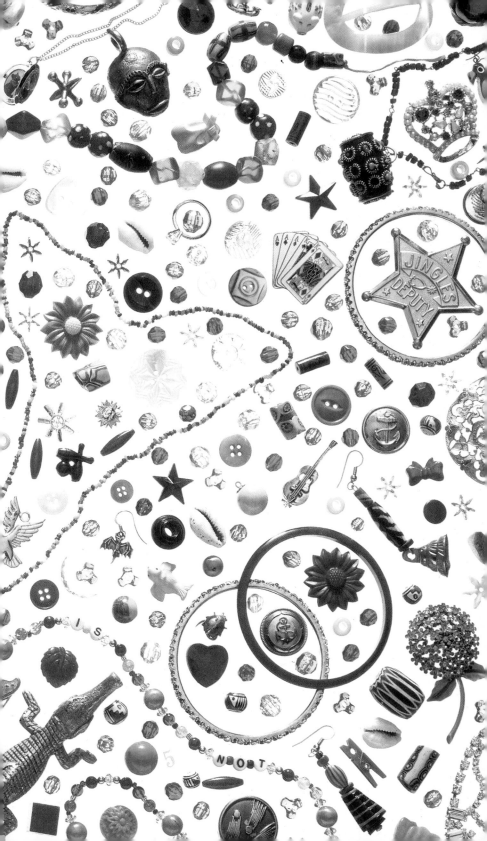

I spy

an eggbeater,

 a blue bowling pin,

a yellow fire hydrant,

and an orange tail fin.

I spy

a timer,

 a frog,

 an E,

a yellow bus,

 and a wooden D.

I spy

a bike,

 a car with a 9,

an 8,

and a truck
with MILK
on a sign.

I spy two matching words.

yellow fire
hydrant

 yellow bus

green star

I spy two matching words.

 face that's small

button that's red

pink stingray

I spy two words that start with the letter C.

corn

five cards

pipe

I spy two words that start with the letters GL.

boxing glove

glasses

scissors

I spy two words that end with the letter N.

 orange tail fin

blue bowling pin

 football

I spy two words that end with the letters ER.

eggbeater

 hammer

nut

I spy two words that rhyme.

duck

 truck

hat

I spy two words that rhyme.

 car with a 9

green star

 badge